What Is My Shadow Made Of?

Questions Kids Ask About Everyday Science

Written by Neil Morris
Illustrated by Mik Brown

READER'S DIGEST
Kids®

Pleasantville, N.Y. • Montreal

Contents

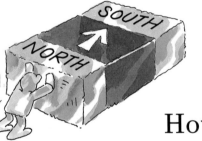

Hi! How many times can you find us in this book?

Why do drums go boom?

All sounds, from big booms on a bass drum to zinging strings on a guitar, are made from vibrations — something shaking back and forth very quickly. When you hit a drum, the drum skin vibrates. When you strum a guitar, the strings vibrate.

Drums make especially loud sounds because the vibrations get trapped inside the drum and bounce back and forth between the drum skins.

4

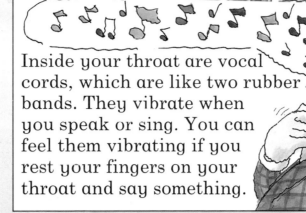

Inside your throat are vocal cords, which are like two rubber bands. They vibrate when you speak or sing. You can feel them vibrating if you rest your fingers on your throat and say something.

Try it yourself!
There's an easy way to see a drum making vibrations. Put some grains of rice on the top of the drum and then tap it gently. The vibrations make the rice dance and jump. If you hit the drum harder, some rice grains may jump right off!

What makes a car go?

When an adult turns the key in a car, the car's engine starts up. The engine turns the wheels and makes the car go by burning a mixture of gasoline and air. Without the key, the engine, or the gas, the car won't go anywhere!

1. Gasoline travels in a pipe from the gasoline tank near the back of the car to the engine.

Gas

Shaft

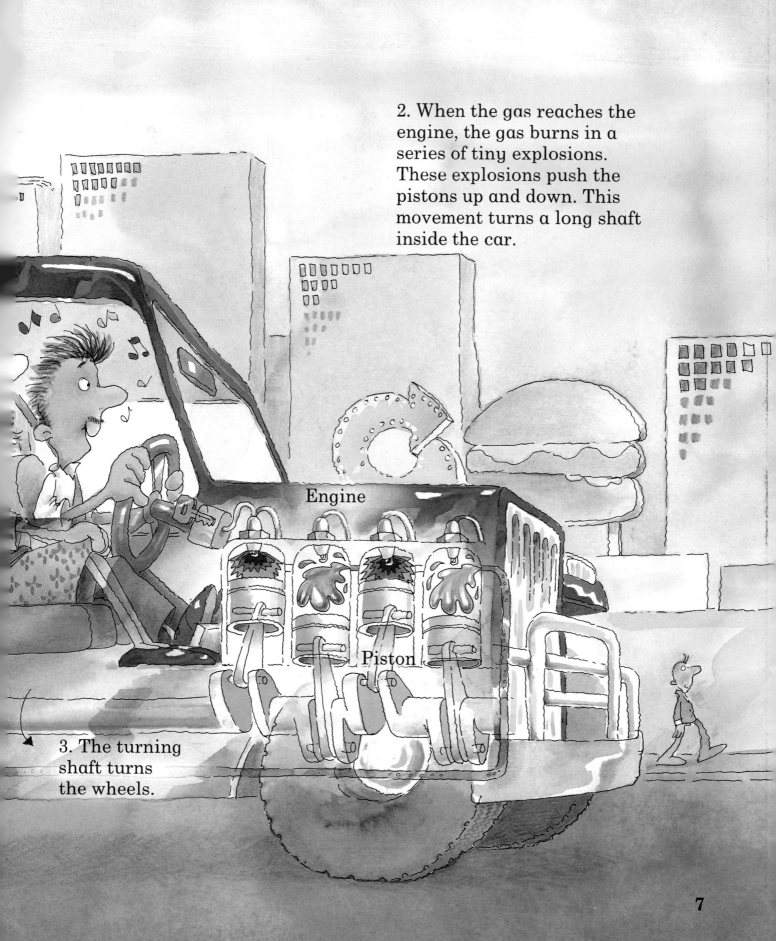

2. When the gas reaches the engine, the gas burns in a series of tiny explosions. These explosions push the pistons up and down. This movement turns a long shaft inside the car.

Engine

Piston

3. The turning shaft turns the wheels.

What is air?

Air is a mixture of invisible gases that is all around you. One of the gases in air is oxygen, which we all need to breathe. Although you can't see air, you can see what it does when you blow air into a balloon. You can feel air in a breeze and hear it when you blow a horn.

Wind is moving air. Sometimes it's strong enough to move other things. What is the wind moving here?

8

Helium balloons fly into the sky because helium is lighter than air.

Hot air is lighter than cold air. Some big balloons are filled with hot air and float up, up, and away!

If you blow up a balloon with air, it falls to the ground because air has weight.

If you were to put all the air in a big room into a balloon, the balloon would weigh about as much as a grown-up!

HELIUM

What is my shadow made of?

Your shadow isn't made of anything — it's just a dark shape. If you try to touch it, all you do is make a different shadow! Shadows are made when something gets in the way of light. So if you get in the path of sunlight, you block out the light and make a shadow.

At high noon, when the sun is directly overhead, the sunlight hits only the top of your body. You block out less light, so your shadow is smaller.

When the sun is low in the sky, your whole body blocks its path, so your shadow is longer.

A bird

A rabbit

A dog

Try it yourself!
You can make your shadow get bigger and smaller. Hold a light behind you so that you can see your shadow on a blank wall.

Move the light closer, then move it farther away. What happens to your shadow?

More shadow pictures to try
Can you make these shadows on your wall?

An elephant

A crocodile

A duck

Shadow pictures

A dark room, someone with a flashlight, and your own two hands are all you need to have fun making shadow pictures on the wall. Can you guess what each one of these will be? (Hint: All are animals!)

Why does my magnet stick to some things?

Your magnet only sticks to things made of metal. And the metal must have iron or nickel in it. Keys and paper clips will stick to the magnet like magic. But things made of wood, plastic, glass, cloth, or rubber will not.

What things can your magnet pick up? Does it pick up *all* metals? Try an aluminum can.

Try it yourself!

The ends of magnets are called poles. Each magnet has a north pole on one end and a south pole on the other.

If you put two magnets with opposite poles near each other, they will pull together. If the same poles are together, the magnets push each other away.

Do you have magnets on your refrigerator? They stick to the door because the door is made of steel, which is a metal with iron in it.

Magnets can make metal things more magnetic. If you hold a paper clip against a magnet, the paper clip will then pick up more paper clips.

How do planes fly?

Planes can fly because they have high-speed engines and specially shaped wings that are curved on the top and flatter underneath. The wings work with the air currents to lift the plane into the sky and keep it there — until the pilot lands it.

Before the plane can take off into the air, it needs to go very fast to force air over the wings. That's why planes use powerful engines to speed down the runway.

Try it yourself!
You can see how a plane wing works by blowing hard across the top of a sheet of paper. The end of the sheet lifts into the air. This is because the air is moving faster over the top of the paper than below it.

Air rushes over and under the wings of a moving plane.

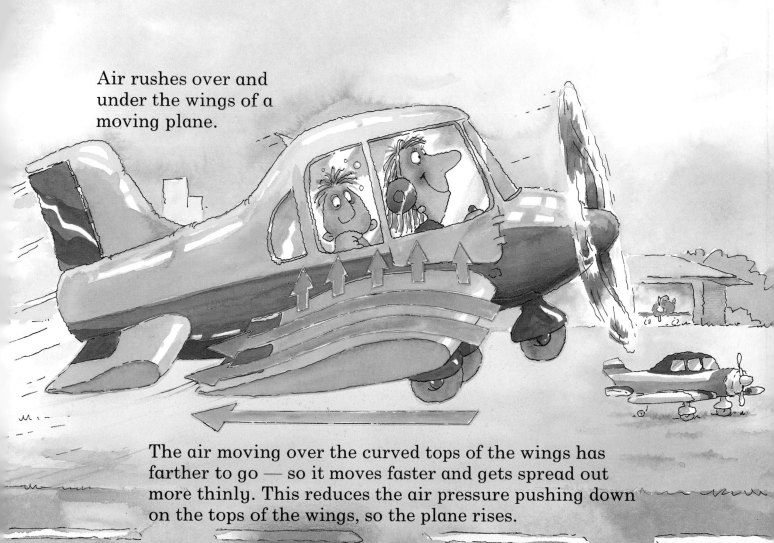

The air moving over the curved tops of the wings has farther to go — so it moves faster and gets spread out more thinly. This reduces the air pressure pushing down on the tops of the wings, so the plane rises.

Why can I see myself in the mirror?

Because of the way light bounces off mirrors — it's like the way a ball bounces off a wall. When you look in a mirror, light first bounces from you onto the shiny surface of the mirror. Then it bounces back from the mirror to your eyes, and you see yourself. What you see is called a reflection.

Light goes straight through clear glass. If you paint glass silver on the back, light will bounce back to you, creating a reflection. This is how a mirror works.

You can have fun with mirrors because they turn things around. If you write your name on a piece of paper and hold it up in front of a mirror, the letters will appear backward in the mirror.

HALL OF MIRRORS

In a hall of mirrors, the mirrors are curved so that light doesn't bounce straight back. It bounces back in different directions, which changes the reflections.

If you stand between two mirrors that face each other, you'll see many reflections. This is because light keeps bouncing back and forth between the two mirrors, creating more and more yous!

17

How many colors are there?

Millions! From lemon yellow to sky blue to pickle green, there are so many colors you can't count them all! That's because you can mix colors together to make new colors. How many colors can you make?

You need only three colors to make lots of other colors. The three main colors are red, yellow, and blue. They are called primary colors.

There are millions of different colors because there are thousands of different shades of each color. Look at this painting. Here are some of the many shades of blue.

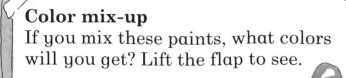
19

What makes things slippery?

Things are slippery because their surfaces are smooth and they slide easily. Just think how slippery new party shoes can be. Sneakers aren't slippery because their soles are rough, and they grip any surface you walk on. The rough soles create friction — a force that stops things from sliding.

Friction is what allows you to grip the rope in a tug-of-war. Without it, the rope would slip right out of your hands!

Without friction, the bow you tied in your shoelace would slip out, and your shoe would slip off.

20

Like the bottoms
of your sneakers,
tires also have
special marks that
keep them from
slipping.

When you squeeze bicycle brakes,
friction between the brakes and
the wheels makes your bike stop.
Without friction, your bike would
roll on forever.

21

How does water get into the faucet?

It starts with rain. First, rain falls into lakes, rivers, and reservoirs. Then it travels through tanks and pipes, being cleaned along the way. Finally, it is pumped through underground pipes into your home, ready at the turn of the faucet.

1. Rain falls from clouds into streams and rivers that flow down to fill a big reservoir.

2. Then the water is cleaned. A chemical called alum is added, and dirt and sand are filtered out.

22

Smaller pipes inside the walls of your home carry the water to your faucets. So it's ready and waiting when you turn it on.

PUMP HOUSE

STORAGE TANK

CHLORINE

FLUORIDE

FLUORIDE

CHLORINE

4. Clean water is then pumped by the pump house through underground pipes to homes and businesses.

3. Chemicals called chlorine and fluoride are also sometimes added to kill germs and help protect your teeth.

Why does my hair stand up when I comb it?

When you comb your hair quickly on a dry day, the comb rubs against the thousands of hairs on your head and makes a kind of electricity called static electricity. That electricity is what makes your hair stand up!

> Positively shocking!

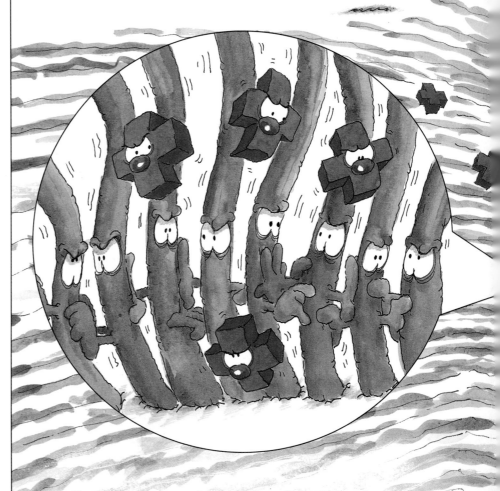

Opposites attract!

Static electricity can be positive (+) or negative (-).

Two positives push each other away.

Two negatives also push each other away.

But one positive and one negative attract each other!

Combing your hair on a dry day gives all the hairs the same positive charge. Each hair tries to push the next one away. When all the hairs are pushing against each other, they all stand up.

Try it yourself!
Here's a magic trick you can do with static electricity. Rub a balloon on a sweater to give it a static charge. Then put one hand on top of the balloon. Surprise! The balloon will stick to your hand. Can you tell why?

Have you ever seen little sparks fly when you take off a sweater in the dark? This is static electricity made by your clothes rubbing together.

How do boats float?

Boats float because of their shape and weight. A boat's weight pushes it down, but the water pushes it up. The boat's weight is spread out over a large area, so the water has a lot to push against. This holds the boat up. But if the boat fills with water, it gets heavier and pushes down harder. Then the boat will sink.

Try it yourself!
Try floating a ball of clay. It sinks because all its weight is in a very small place. There's not much for the water to push against. If you take the same clay and make it into a boat shape, it will float.

The shape of a boat helps it push a lot of water out of the way. The water that is pushed away pushes back against the boat and holds it up.

The apple, sponge, and wooden spoon will float because they are full of air and don't weigh much for their size.

The metal spoon, the coins, and the pebbles will sink. They don't have much air inside and are heavy for their size. What happens to a metal bowl?

You can feel how strongly water pushes up. Push a ball underwater and then let it go. The water will push the ball right up into the air!

27

Can the people on TV see me?

You can see them, but they can't see you! They are in a TV studio and all they can see are the cameras and crew. The camera tapes the show. Then the show is broadcast to your home. So when a funny clown says, "I'll see you next week!" what he means is, "You'll see *me* next week!"

2. The signals move along a wire to a transmitter. Each signal carries a piece of the picture.

1. The TV camera changes the clown's picture into electric signals.

3. At the transmitter, the signals are made stronger and sent out into the air.

4. The antenna on your roof picks up the signals and sends them down a wire to your TV set.

5. The TV changes the signals back into pictures and sound. On with the show!

Why do things fall down instead of up?

Because of gravity. Gravity is an invisible force that pulls everything on earth downward. When you throw something up in the air, gravity soon pulls it back down. The moon has gravity too, but much less. Look at the difference gravity can make!

Thanks to gravity, there is only one way to go from the top of a slide — down.

When you throw a ball up, gravity is what brings it back down again.

You can bounce high on a trampoline, but you always come straight back down — because of gravity!

The moon has less
gravity than earth
because the moon is
much smaller.

A slide on the moon
wouldn't be much
fun. You would slide
down, but very slowly.

If you were on the moon and tossed
a ball up, it would take a long time
to come down because there's not
much gravity pulling on it.

Imagine a trampoline
on the moon. You
would bounce six
times as high as you
do on earth.

31

A Reader's Digest Kids Book
Published by The Reader's Digest Association, Inc.
Produced by Larousse plc

Copyright © 1995, 1994 Larousse plc

Library of Congress Cataloging in Publication Data

Morris, Neil.
   What is my shadow made of? : questions kids ask about everyday
science / Neil Morris ; illustrations by Mik Brown. — Trade ed.
   p.   cm. — [Tell me why]
   ISBN 0-89577-609-X.
   1. Science — Miscellanea — Juvenile literature.   [2. Science —
Experiments — Juvenile literature. [1. Science — Miscellanea.
2. Science — Experiments. 3. Experiments 4. Questions and
answers.] I. Brown, Mik, ill. II. Title. III. Series.
Q163.M887 1995
500 — dc20   94-14120
                                                    CIP
                                                    AC

Reader's
Digest

Reader's Digest, the Pegasus logo, and Reader's Digest Kids and design are
registered trademarks, and Tell Me Why is a trademark,
of The Reader's Digest Association, Inc.

Printed in Hong Kong

2 4 6 8 10 9 7 5 3 1